17 Days To Your Own Profitable Home Watch Business

A Step-By-Step Success Manual

Mark Mehling

"The Home Watch Guy"

The 39page guide *series is your shortcut to expert information. You could spend hours searching the web and still not find the information you have here in a simple, easy to read, short summary. Each book provides a solid foundation that saves you a ton of time and fruitless hunting.*

If you want more intense information, see if there is a 59page *or* 79page guide *book available.*

Keep in mind our goal:
> *Easy to read, less than 2 hours for the average reader*
> *At least 36 pages of information*
> *Few if any pretty pictures*
> *Quick to understand, distilled to be readable and informative immediately*
> *Written by an expert for those with little or no knowledge.*
> *More than an overview but less than a compendium*
> *an offer for more information from the author (optional)*

If you want to get to the meat of a topic quickly, 39pageguidebooks *make that happen.*

If you like fat filled, long explanations, 'technical jargon', and lots of space used up by pictures, these books are NOT for you.

FORWARD

Congratulations! You have taken the first step to opening your own business, a home watch service.

Just so it is clear from the beginning, I am a successful Home Watch business owner. I am not a lawyer, accountant, or insurance agent. I am providing the best information I have available and researched, but none of this can be construed to be legal, accounting, tax, or insurance advice. Because every state (and city and county) has different rules and laws, you need to use a professional for these areas that can address your specific situation.

You agree, by buying this book, to release the author, publisher, and all other parties from all liability for any action you may/may not take based on the contents. Basically, you are assuming all the liability. In some circles, that means you alone are personally accountable- a novel concept from the past that seems to be absent today. But I digress.

Let's start by answering a few questions that pop up all the time:

Why is now a great time to start your own Home Watch Business?

There is a huge migration starting with the retirees moving to warmer climates for the cold season. But they still want to be near families and friends part of the year and are affluent enough to have two houses. Besides, who want to live in the heat of Arizona or Florida in the summer? These are smarter people who know the risks of leaving a home empty and want a qualified person to watch the house.

This service is new, replacing using friends and neighbors who are not qualified to watch the house, don't have the time (everybody is working nowadays), and feel imposed on.

People aren't as emotionally close as they used to be, are busier, and don't want the responsibility of someone else's house.

What is a home watch service?

A home watch service maintains the property to a certain level, surveys the property on a scheduled basis and after any event that could cause damage (storms, hurricanes, power outages, earthquakes, etc.). A professional home watch service is properly insured and licensed. It also meets other standards to differentiate it from 'the neighbor next door.'

A homeowner will hire a home watch professional when they recognize the investment they have in their home, and know the difference between friends or neighbors and a professional service. One of the key elements of a new home watch service is training potential clients on the difference.

What isn't a home watch service?

A Home watch service IS NOT a security service. DO NOT present it this way. You can present it as a way to keep the inside of the house protected from bugs, failed appliances and water damage. But do not suggest in any way that this is a security service. Why?

Several reasons:
    -you are not a service that will contact the authorities real time meaning when an event is happening.
    -you do not/cannot automatically respond when there is a burglary. Sure, you can be added as a person to call when there is a problem at the house, but someone responding to an alarm at a central station does this
    -you do not know the status of the burglar alarm from where

you are (unless you are inside the house or just set the alarm.) -you are not insured as a security service (see insurance section)

A Home Watch Service is NOT a home inspection service.
You can have a home watch service AND a home inspection service but the two are completely different. Your clients need to know that you are different from a home inspection service if there is the slightest confusion.

A Home Inspection service will crawl around attics, and make other detailed INSPECTIONS. I personally use the term 'survey' to avoid confusion in the mind of my clients. You *survey* the various systems but do not go in-depth for the purposes of evaluating their installation, etc. You DO an operational check of the various systems and make sure the house and grounds meet other requirements a home inspector could care less about.

For example, a home inspector could care less about mail in the mailbox, flyers on the door, and garbage and weeds in the flowerbeds.

On the other hand, a home watch service doesn't care if the ceiling fans are installed according to code, the number of cross members in the attic ceiling is correct, or the amount of insulation is adequate for the job.

This includes NOT being responsible (as a home watch service) for pest in the attic or other places that are not normally seen in the course of walking through a house. There are various services who specialize in these areas. They are trained and insured, and in some states licensed, to do this type work. You are not!

A Home Watch service is NOT house sitting.
House sitting is a completely separate concept where someone lives in the property in the absence of the owner. A home watch service does not live in the property, does not arrange to have someone live in the property and does not recommend people to live in the property. If someone is looking for a house sitter, they need to look

elsewhere.

A home watch service is NOT, <u>by most definitions,</u> a 'property manager'.
You are in fact, a property manager for an individual, but you have to be careful with words here. The standard definition for a property manager refers to a *COMMERCIAL* property manager. A *commercial* property manager accepts rents, arranges tenants, signs contracts with tenants, and other functions that almost always requires a state license. And a lot of training and testing.

By avoiding these specific tasks- finding tenants, accepting money for the owner(s), and signing contracts or arranging contracts between the owner and third parties, you can avoid the restrictions that make a state license required.

If you are already a property manager, I personally recommend separating the function for your home watch service to avoid any connection between the two job descriptions. The insurance requirements are very different and you should arrange your work such that 'never the twain shall meet.' Even your accountant will recommend this.

Remember, I am not a lawyer. Every state is different. But my research has shown that you do not need a license to watch privately owned homes as long as you are only dealing with the owner, do not arrange tenants or accept rents. Some states refer to this as having a 'fiduciary' relationship, meaning you are trusted with someone else's money and are responsible for handling that person's business affairs. By avoiding this situation, you establish your home watch business as an unregulated service that does not require a real estate license, or a property manager's license.

QUICK ANSWER GUIDE

Can anyone start a home watch business?

In a word, yes. This is a perfect opportunity to start part time while you are working another job, an excellent second source of income for retirees looking for something to stay busy.

Do I need to be a home inspector?

No. In fact, it may work against you to be a licensed home inspector. Why? Because what you are accomplishing as a Home Watch business is NOT what a home inspector would necessarily do. You will not be crawling in attics, preparing massive reports, nor giving people information that could affect the sales price of a home. If you are a home inspector, you should ensure you separate out the two businesses so there is no confusion. Some knowledge of homes, how they operate, and what to look for is very helpful but can be learned by anyone willing to put the time and effort into a little research and reading.

Do I need to be a handyman?

If you have any questions about the risks that an empty home can cause a homeowner, you need to buy my book "leaving Your Home-ALONE" which outlines, in over 200 pages, the challenges, and solutions, for an empty home. The book is written for homeowners but makes an excellent foundation for those looking for the problems they must overcome in an empty house. It will give you ideas as a new business owner for services that you can offer to your new clients that other services do not.

But to answer the question more directly, a handyman has certain advantages, but you don't have to actually be handy at all. If you can use checklists, have attention to detail, and use the right tools, you can hire a handyman to fix many of the minor problems you will come across in the course of looking at homes.

If you are a handyman, all the better. There are many times that simple small fixes, for which you charge the client, can be accomplished if you have some experience.

It all depends how you want to operate- by doing everything yourself, or by managing the properties using others when it would take you more time than it is worth.

Can I start with no money?

Essentially, you have already spent money if you are reading this. Can you start this business with a SMALL amount of money- yes. No money? Not really. You will need insurance, should form a company, do some marketing, should invest in a few courses or books, and need some cash for expenses until you start getting money from clients. You have the opportunity to get a thriving home watch business by investing as little as $2,000-3,000 over a couple months for insurance, basic marketing, and courses. Compared to the cheapest franchise, this is peanuts.

You can try to re-invent everything yourself, but that is fool's work and will mean it will take, on average, 5 times longer to have a thriving business. You will be investing a tremendous amount of time, ignoring the experience of those who have gone before you, and will probably make huge financial and operational mistakes.

A couple hundred dollars invested in checklists, recommended tools, and other shortcuts will allow you to be up and running much quicker than trying to come up with everything on your own.

The choice is certainly yours. Very few businesses in any industry ever grow when the owner spends his time re-creating what he could easily buy. Time is really money. A single missed item on a checklist that you created yourself, could cost you the client or worse, the entire business. Be smart and use what others have already created. You don't build your own car, you buy one pre-made. It is the same for a business.

Where do I find customers or clients?

Empty houses are everywhere, however, I believe there are three basic sources:
>-Vacationers or Snowbirds (Seasonal residents)
>-Homes left empty that are For Sale
>-Homes left empty when the owner has moved to assisted living or has passed away. (More common in warm states than northern ones).

Of these, seasonal residents are the predominant source.

What insurance do I need?

Although you will be using general business insurance, you must specifically get a policy that covers a home watch service. Because the industry is relatively young, few insurance agents know how to contact the limited number of providers. Uninformed insurance agents will sell you the wrong insurance, leaving you open to liability. The most common mistakes are agents selling *(and poorly informed business owners buying)*:

>-Handyman Insurance
>-Property Management insurance
>-Security Service Insurance
>-Lawn Care provider insurance
>-Professional Liability Insurance also called 'Errors and Omissions' Insurance

There are companies that specifically sell "Home Watch" business insurance. Unfortunately, because of the way the insurance business operates, I cannot give you the name of an agent or insurance company that you can use. Agents only represent certain companies, and companies may only sell insurance in certain states. To add to the confusion, there is a middleman between the agents and insurance company called by various names, such as an aggregator, who also plays a part. This is one area where research on your part will be necessary.

Simple part: make sure you have Home Watch insurance, and your policy CLEARLY states that it is a policy for a business in the Home

Watch Industry.

How much does yearly insurance cost?

Although there is not a simple answer for this question, expect to pay $800- $1,000 a year during the initial stages. If you are paying substantially MORE or LESS, there is probably a problem.

If you are paying a lot more, you may have insurance that you do not need. Why pay for insurance that is not required?

If you are paying a lot less, you probably don't have the proper coverage. Without proper coverage, you are risking the entire business for one simple mistake.

Read the section on insurance to get a better understanding, but being over or under-insured is a dangerous situation that could claim your business as well as possibly result in a devastating lawsuit that could take your personal property. (Don't forget to read the disclaimer at the beginning of the book.)

Why do you use 'client' instead of 'customer' in this book?

Although many people use client and customer as if they had the same meaning, they do not. A customer is a person who buys one time. That's the end of the connection between the buyer and seller. Now the seller looks for another person to buy their product or service. Think of going into most big box hardware stores and buying a hammer for cash. Once you leave, there is no evidence that you were there, they do not offer to send you sale flyers. No one asks your name.

Clients on the other hand, are usually given that title in relationships intended to last a lifetime. Lawyers have clients. Financial experts have clients. They are in a position to be an influence for a lifetime. In this case, the client places a tremendous trust in the service provider. This is exactly the same relationship you need to build in the home watch business. You don't want just a customer; you want someone who comes under your personal care and protection for the life of the relationship. This is especially important because you will have clients who, because of the trust you have built, will stay with your service for many years.

Is this an instant moneymaker and guaranteed success?
If you are looking for that lottery ticket job, where you work for an hour and retire with millions, keep looking. This book will not be able to help you. This entire book, and other courses available, can give you are the tools to get going. There is no way to determine how hard you want to work, or whether you actually did what was in the book or course.

This is not a lottery ticket but a toolbox. The toolbox contains the tools but they have no effect on your income or success if you fail to take them out and use them as intended.

I cannot guarantee success, but I do guarantee that the contents of this book were gathered over 7 years of active service with the leading service in the industry.

How to use this book
This book is conveniently divided by days. If you find that you need more time, just consider these to be steps. On the other hand, if you finish a day and want to get started on the next day, go for it! There is a make-up day in the middle in case you get behind. Some steps may be harder for you than others, no problem. One other point- once you establish your business, there are two ongoing items that you must do every day- staying in the conversation and marketing for the future.

Both of these receive special attention.

NOTES:

DAY 1

Unless you are super savvy with a portable computer or smart phone, your best bet is to get a notebook to keep track of all the different things you will research and discover.

Although everything is important in the business, there is nothing as important as getting customers or clients. You can have business cards, a great plan, nice uniforms, and the entire paperwork perfect, but without money coming in, you don't have an ongoing business. Today you begin your research.

To determine if there is a real need for a home watch service, do the following:

1. Drive around your area looking at empty houses. Not abandoned ones- at least not yet. You are looking to see if there are houses that the owners are not living in for months at a time. Record the addresses; you will use this information later.

2. Contact all your friends and family and tell them that you are considering opening this business. Ask for everyone they know that leaves their home empty for the summer or winter. These are all potential candidates for your service. Record their names and addresses. If you don't know their address, you will be able to look that up later using tax records or other sources.

3. See if the tax records for your area are available online. With very few exceptions, this should be easy to do by looking up your local tax office, real estate tax assessor, or similar name. Once on the site, see if you can find the mailing address for the owner of a house you looked at in step 1. If the owner uses an out of town address, you may have a lead.

NOTE: You may be able to have the tax office compile a list for a small fee. If you look at the tax records and then ask your local tax office to isolate addresses and names based on the entries, it can save a lot of time in your marketing. For example, asking for the names and addresses of everyone in a particular zip code whose house is valued over $300K, send their tax bills out of state, are are listed as non-residents can provide a nice list.

4. Contact insurance agents and see if they have clients that leave empty homes behind. They may be relieved to find someone they can recommend, as it will dramatically cut insurance company losses and the insurance agents hassles.

5. Consider other 'people of influence' that see empty houses every day. These may include plumbers, air conditioning people, security people. Each of them may also be able to relate stories that you can use in your sales presentation.

6. Contact Assisted Living and funeral homes to see if they have clients who have had to leave homes behind. They may be an excellent source of leads for houses that are now handled by the kids because Mom and Dad are in an assisted living facility or, in the case of a funeral home, there are out of state heirs that could use professional services.

7. Contact real estate agents and brokers. Many have empty homes for sale that should receive regular attention to prevent damage and affect the possible sale. Most agents are too busy and completely untrained in watching homes. Smart brokers realize the risk they take with an empty home for sale. They can easily pass the cost on to the seller and you can save them lawsuits, lost sales, and angry homeowners.

The list of names you have developed now becomes the basis for your marketing, which will occur, in another step on another day.

NOTES:

DAY 2

Congratulations! You have started to build a successful business! You can pat yourself on the back because 90% of all the people who ever say they are going to start a business never pass the talking stage. You have already made progress.
Choosing the form of your business and Competitors

Competitors- Who are your competitors?

Understanding the competition is very important. No one goes into combat expecting to use judo against an enemy that uses roadside bombs or IEDs (Improvised Explosive Devices).

Today's mission is to gather as much information as possible about the competition so that you know who they are and how they operate. Only then can you make a decision about how to exploit their weakness and thus empower your own service.

Two main groups constitute your competitors- (1) friends and neighbors and (2) other home watch services.

Because this concept is relatively new, you may find that the biggest competitor to your success is NOT another business. It is the neighbor, relatives, or people who actually just leave the house empty. Part of today's work is to embrace this reality and start the thinking that will allow you to overcome this competition.

The first part of overcoming any competition is understanding who they are, what they do, how they do it, *and how you can do it better.* Do you immediately know and understand the difference between a taxi and a limo? If you establish your service like this, where the difference is obvious, you won't have to deal with the lower level competition as much.

So begin to think how you can separate yourself so dramatically that the difference is obvious. If someone is searching for transportation and offered a bicycle versus a limo, the difference is so obvious they know immediately which they want.

Because people establish relationships with neighbors, your best bet may be approaching the newest buyers in the area. Remember this when you start marketing.

Your homework is to start thinking how you will be different than friends and neighbors.

When your competition is another business:

The first rule of thumb that has served me well came from my brother Jim. I had done the research back in 2004 and found a total of three other services in the entire web. However, as I laid everything out, having to create everything because there were no services or courses to copy or buy, more people started to enter the business. I was concerned until my brother reassured me with this great advice:
"There is always room for someone to do it better."

Don't be discouraged by competition. In fact, you need competition so that you can be compared, and hopefully, be seen as the much better option. But you still need to understand who your competition is. How to do that?

Start by looking for websites for other services. Look through every link on their site.

-Do they show prices? (Big mistake!). Understand their pricing structure. Most services that show this information are grossly undercharging and will eventually leave the business because the time invested compared to the profit received is so small.

-Do they show their checklist? You can use this as a starting point. But if you want to do better than they are doing, you need a

comprehensive checklist that convinces potential clients you know what you are doing. (And when you get your checklist, don't ever post it on a website, another big mistake.

-Also look for what services they offer, any information about credit cards they accept, and other features of their business. See how professional they look in pictures. Do they have uniforms? *(Look in Chapter 16 of my book "Leaving Your Home-ALONE" for the best list of services that should be offered.)*

If there isn't a website for a service, that says a whole lot. In today's connected world, everyone (including you!) need at least a basic information website.

Forming Your Company

You may be thinking- why do I need to form a company? The answer is very simple- to protect yourself from losing everything you own. Make sense? Ok, let's dig deeper.

If you open a home watch service, you have to establish who is liable for the actions that business performs. That means if the business screws up or is sued, someone must be responsible. The law recognizes some types of businesses as being a legal entity (they are treated as a person), while other forms, specifically a Sole Proprietorship, makes the owner fully liable.

Think of a business like IBM. Should you decide to sue IBM, you would be suing the company, not individuals. The Company is treated like a person and becomes liable, thus freeing the individuals from personal responsibility.

You want a business format that protects your personal assets just as IBM employees are protected.

(Remember that I am not a lawyer, just someone trying you help you understand a little of the law.)

You can get the same benefits as IBM. You can separate your personal assets like your home and car, from the company. So if the 'company' screws up and is sued, only the assets of the company can be lost- not your personal property like your home and vehicle.

This is the biggest difference between Sole Proprietorship and other forms of business such as an LLC, S or C Corporation.

Sole proprietorship is considered exclusively owned, operated, and full responsibility assumed by the owner. The owner and the business are viewed as the same 'person' by the legal system.

LLCs, S Corporations and C Corporations are recognized as individual 'persons' separately from the owner or shareholders. So a Sole Proprietorship named Mark Mehling's Home Watch Service could be held liable for damage and my *personal* belongings (car, boat, computers, etc) are up for grabs.

However, formed as an LLC, S Corp or C Corp, the *BUSINESS* would be sued, not necessarily me personally. Again, I am not a lawyer and you should consult one for questions instead of relying entirely on my untrained answers here. But these are the basics.

I personally prefer an LLC. Limited Liability Company(s) (LLC) are recognized as a separate legal entity. Therefore, you are behind a 'veil' that protects what you own personally, such as houses and cars, from the greedy hands of someone after your business. Plus they are easy to form. For even more protection, many entrepreneurs choose C and S Corporations.

There are thousands of pages of research, but I have found this set of links to provide the best explanations. I do not receive any money should you choose to use the services on these pages. I have used them very successfully in the past compared to other 'zoom' sites. Whether you use their services or not, the information is valuable for making a decision and I encourage you to understand each type before choosing.

http://www.bizfilings.com/wizard.aspx

This is a great way to select a few simple answers and let the experts point you toward a specific type of corporate structure.

http://www.bizfilings.com/comparison.aspx
Wonder what the difference is between an LLC, S and C Corporations? Another simple to understand format, although it sounds a little legalese for beginnings.

http://www.bizfilings.com/states.aspx
Wonder how your state views different entities? This is the page that allows you to see exactly what your state requires, which is much better than me trying to list 50 different interpretations.

NOTES:

DAY 3

Do you need a License?

This area, in particular, varies from state to state, as well as county or city.

But there is a significant difference you need to understand, since you may have to explain it to everyone from insurance underwriters to antagonistic real estate people.

There are two types of licenses I am talking about. First is a general business license, which is the local government's way of monitoring your activities. Secondly, a 'professional' license, such as a property manager's license, which requires a course of instruction, testing, and ongoing fees paid to the state.

Most cities and counties, and some states, do have a general business license that you are required to obtain. In Florida, it is less than $50 a year and the most expensive state I have heard of, New York, is less than $100. This notifies local authorities that you are an active business. Anyone looking on the tax records will want to know that you are registered. Most insurance companies will not sell you a policy if you are not licensed. Remember seeing 'licensed and bonded' on a service provider's truck? There is every possibility the word 'license' means a general business license.

However, as this is written, I am not aware of a single state that requires a 'professional' license for you to operate a home watch service. The emphasis here is on the word 'professional' because you will probably need at least a general business license from a local agency. But certain trades people and professionals are required to be licensed by the state. These may include doctors, lawyers, real estate sales people and brokers, commercial property managers, builders, plumbers, electricians, etc.

In my experience, and I recommend you consult a lawyer or do your own research, the difference between a home watch service and a 'property manager', for licensing purposes, is the placing of tenants and collection of rent money. There is a legal term, 'fiduciary responsibility', that applies to property managers and does not apply to you as long as you do not place tenants in properties and absolutely do not handle rent money in any form. Avoiding this critical element will keep you clean and away from the courthouse.

You will find that I use a different language to ensure there is never a connection between my home watch service and other trades. I do not 'inspect' homes. That would, to those who do not know the difference, suggest that I am some form of a home inspector. Since this is a *licensed occupation*, I do not want this association with my work.

Additionally, potential clients who have experience with home inspectors (almost all of them) will, in their mind, assume I am doing a home inspection in the course of my work. I do not want this misconception either. While a home inspector crawls through attics, checking for roof leaks, I do not. A home inspector writes reports, takes hundreds of pictures, and essentially certifies the systems in the house. I do not and you won't either. So this separation is very important. (As an aside, I refer to 'surveys' of the property, not inspections.)

Once you have your business license, you are absolutely entitled to answer the question "Are you licensed?" with a confident "Yes!" Most homeowners have no clue what the different licensing requirements are. You have fulfilled the minimum licensing requirements- and a whole lot more than their friends and neighbors.

NOTES:

DAY 4

Choosing a Name

If you chose the form of your business as Sole Proprietorship, most states require your personal name to be part of the business name. "Smith's Barbecue" could act as your business name without a lot of other work. But, if you have read this far, you know I am absolutely opposed to having a sole proprietorship. In my opinion, only a fool will set up his home watch business this way, even temporarily.

For everyone else, you can choose any name you want. Here are some guidelines:

Pick a name that is easily remembered. 'Billy Bob's Bug Busters and Beatle Blasters" may sound cool but will be hard for clients to remember. Same for "Harry's Heavenly Home Watch and House Sitting and Repair Service".

Consider a name that also has the world wide web domain name available. This will be very helpful when you set up your web site.

Use a name that conveys some clue to what you do. "Martha's Residential Vacancy Management Services" is probably too confusing to most snowbirds- your primary clients.

There are many arguments for and against certain types of names. I believe you should put what you do in the name somewhere. It can be in a 'tagline' but I think this is a mistake. You can look at many names of huge companies and have no clue what they do. For example, VOCUS® is a company. Can you tell me what they do from looking solely at the name? Unless you have millions of dollars to invest (like they have), you can't afford to have potential clients seeing your name and wondering what you do. Because we are early into this industry, there may be people who still don't know what "Lakeside Home Watch Service" really does, but they have an idea in their mind. On the other hand, "Homeowner Services Company" will probably confuse most people because it is completely unclear what is offered.

Personal name selection

In the past, using your name in the business name was common. The world was much smaller, and a lot of people were known in the town. Thus, "Pete's Garage" was well known because everyone knew Pete. Today, people may not necessarily want a 'small' sounding name like that. Besides, if you ever expect to grow and use other people, it may confuse potential clients who "Pete" or "Bob" or "Tina" really is. The choice is yours, there are certainly advantages if a lot of people know you and you will be the face of the company in all circumstances. But I lean away from that method.

Geographic name selection

Obviously, you may want to choose a name that reflects your service area. This is a two edged sword. This tells people 'that service is for me' if they live in that area, but unless you use a very broad area, it also eliminates those who may believe your service doesn't cover their area. For example, if you have "Mainstreet Home Watch" who knows what your area of service really is. Or "Smithtown Home Watch". Do you do own a house *outside* of Smithtown?

Whatever name you select, you can then go online and create your own logo and business cards, or hire a professional. One of my favorite websites for services like this is http://www.vistaprint.com" **www.vistaprint.com**. I do not receive any income from recommending you to this site, but have found it inexpensive and easy to use. More information on this on Day 8.

Your homework today is to find a website or vendor you like and start the paperwork to form your business from what you learned in the previous chapter.

NOTES:

DAY 5

Tools

If you haven't started researching all the tools necessary to do your job right, now is the time to start. As a minimum, consider flashlights, a ladder, temperature and humidity sensors, specific tools to turn water and gas on/off, and a camera to record problems. Also a simple set of hand tools like screwdrivers and wrenches will come in handy.

Uniforms

You might ask: why would we need a uniform, we are only going into empty houses, right? But a simple uniform commands a lot of respect from clients as well as other business people.

Think of the effect of a uniform on your attitude. If policemen wore Hawaiian shirts, would they be as effective? Have you ever heard that women still fall in love with a man in a uniform? Well, you don't need to dress in Navy Blue uniforms with stripes on your sleeve and a tie so stop worrying.

But simple, standard uniforms can make a real difference in perception about your business and you or your employees. You can buy a simple white shirt with either long or short sleeves with your company name or logo embroidered above the left pocket for less than $20 apiece, sometimes a whole lot less. Combined with a simple pair of Dockers® style pants and work shoes, it still looks a lot more professional than your competition. You can use any color dark pants and the outfit looks professional, attractive, and isn't very expensive. If you want to top it off with a ballcap with your name embroidered, these are less than $10, even in smaller quantities.

My best choice here is **www.Queensboro.com**. Do this after you have done your logo.

NOTES:

DAY 6

Insurance and Accounting

As mentioned in the opening section and FAQs, your business must be insured for many reasons. The biggest is to avoid lawsuits should a problem arise that you could be considered at fault.

Today's environment, which has little or no personal responsibility, is 'sue happy'. I am in the same boat so must again note that I am not a licensed insurance agent and everything here should be worked through someone legally empowered. But here's the important stuff from personal experience.

Insurance- the home watch industry is still small and most insurance agents have no idea how to get the appropriate insurance. You will need to contact multiple agents to get a business insurance policy specifically for 'home watch' services.

Bonding

The phrase 'bonded and insured' gives reassurance to many potential clients. Most, however, have no clue what it really means.

Bonding or a bond is an agreement (that you pay for) from a company that agrees to pay your clients for items they believe have been stolen or damaged. The company holding the bond pays your clients and then goes after you for the money! It's not insurance. And here are some key points:

> -you don't need to be bonded if you (or you and your spouse) are the sole employee. Bonding is for your employees. If you are only one, you are responsible as an owner and don't need to be bonded.
> -your local state agency that covers taxation may be able to help with bonding, when you hire other employees.

Liability Insurance

What can you be held liable for? Many things, including
  -damage caused by your negligence (toilet overflows that
  happen after you leave because it didn't shut off and you
  didn't notice, for instance)
  -reasonable care of the home. If you forget to lock the door
  or set the burglar alarm, you could be responsible.
  -damage caused by your 'incompetence'. For example, not
  realizing the toilet has backed up because you didn't do your
  survey properly.

These examples are just that- examples. But the idea is you could be
held liable and, should your client get a judgment, resulting in
bankruptcy for the business as well as you personally. That's why
you need insurance (and a proper business model which, hopefully,
you established on Day 2.)

Professional Liability (or Errors and Omissions) Insurance. This is
for Doctors, Lawyers and Real Estate Agents. NOT for home watch.
Professional liability is very expensive and some agents may claim
you need it. They are wrong. This is the equivalent of malpractice
insurance. Since you are not licensed (like doctors lawyers and real
estate agents), this is not the insurance you need.

Other types
Agents will try to sell you anything, and many will claim it is what
you need. Like the FAQ discusses, ensure you are not sold the wrong
type of insurance. I have purchased, for over 8 years, 'Home Watch'
insurance. But agents have tried to sell me insurance for a security
company, a handyman service, a commercial property management
company, and even a lawn care business! They are clueless as to
what you do and few will take the effort to understand and then get
the correct coverage.

Buy the wrong coverage and it's the same as having NO coverage.

Accounting
When you first get started, you may want to do a simple cash method
of accounting- counting cash in and cash out. Now is the time to get
everything set up properly.

I bill at the *beginning* of the month for (1) the monthly fee in advance and (2) for any other expenses that occurred the *previous* month.

You will need to use a simple service like QuickBooks online, or if you want to do it all by hand, have a system for recording income and expenses.

Almost anything you spend on the business, including getting it established, is an expense to the business. You usually start with a certain amount of money, referred to as capital, for the opening balance. Money collected in fees or for other services is one side while expenses from your vehicle to marketing costs are subtracted. If you are not at all savvy with a checkbook, consider using someone who is. As you get larger, you definitely should use accounting software and keep track of all expenses and income closely to avoid IRS problems.

NOTES:

DAY 7

Contracts

For many clients, your business is a new service and they may not be familiar with what you do. Building rapport is extremely important.

One way to ensure they are not scared off by long term commitments is to change the language from 'contract' to 'service agreement'. It will look like a contract, and if you let a lawyer see it or touch it, it WILL look like a tax form with small lettering and tons of lame writing.

What do you need in a simple contract? Remembering that I am not a lawyer, and this is not legal advice, consider these points:

> **Information-** Names, addresses, emails and phone numbers for both home and 'away'
> **Agreement-** price, possibly billing information (in advance, for instance), credit card info, terms of payment
> Signatures and date
> **Exceptions-** you outline what is not involved, such as 'home inspection', etc.
> **Other points**, like your lost key policy, how you will contact them when there is a problem, etc.
> *Copy for you and them.*

Your contract should use language like 'survey' or 'visits' to emphasize your difference from other service providers.

Your homework is to decide how to do your Service Agreement. There are many printers that can do multipart forms so look around your city or town and see they can do. You can build the form yourself using any computer program like Microsoft Excel, Word, or PowerPoint.

NOTES:

DAY 8

Website domain name

You will probably want at least two domains to get started. The first should be a form of the company name. The second should be the common phrase that people would use to find your business, like the headers in the yellow pages. So if your company name was Best Home Watch, you should try to find a domain name very close, such as besthomewatch.com or BHW.com. You should also research your area to find what search terms people are using to find services like yours and get that domain name, too. So if 'Happauge home watch service" is the predominant search term www.happaugehomewatch.com would be your second domain.

Try to avoid:

Domain names that are difficult or can be misread
www.Whereeveryonegoes.com is especially hard to read.

What do you see when you read the website name for Speed of Art?
www.speedofart.com (what is a 'speedo-fart'?)

And this site, which may have changed before this was printed, which tells who represents which celebrities:
"http://www.whorepresents.com" **www.whorepresents.com** (What did you see immediately?)???

Misspelled names that will let people looking for you end up elsewhere

You can buy a domain name from many places. But I recommend godaddy.com if you have never done it before. Too many places will give you a 'free' domain name when you buy their service. Problem is they own that name and you won't ever be able to change providers. If this all sounds confusing, do some outside research.

This book is not written to teach you about doing websites, but about a home watch service.

Website
Before you ask, yes, you need a website. You can do one of your own without a problem. The key is to be able to show something to those searching digitally. Many people will be out of town when the search and the web is their first choice. My favorite place to get a free website is "http://www.weebly.com" **www.weebly.com**. Not the most powerful or fancy, but easy to do by yourself.

Logos and Administrative Items
Although getting clients is MUCH more important than business cards and letterhead, you should look into these at some point. Logos can be made online very inexpensively. Even hiring someone should be less than $300 for a beautiful set of files that can be used on your website and in graphic programs for advertising, business cards, and brochures.

Consider creating a logo first so you can use it with everything else. If you can use any of the common graphics programs you can add you logo to anything. Designing your own letterhead with your new logo can be fun but keep in mind- your goal is more clients, not pretty business cards.

One of my best sources for business cards, including logos, is Vistaprint.com.

Phone Number
You need to be available by phone. I DO NOT recommend a home phone number. Use your cell phone. You can also invest in an 800 number for a reasonable amount if you want to look especially impressive.

Answering message
When you decide which number to use, immediately change the answering message to sound professional. Singing kids, rap music, and dogs barking do not make it sound like you are serious. If it

takes 15 times to record, do it. And don't use a canned choice. My favorite one, which I copied from someone else, is something like "Hi, this is Mark. I am in a meeting or talking with another client. As a courtesy I have turned off my phone. Please leave a message and I will give you this same courtesy, my undivided attention, when I return your call. If you don't leave a message, I won't know you called…"

NOTES:

DAY 9

Catch up day

You can use this day to catch up if you have fallen behind. If you don't need this as an additional day, it is equally important to relax. Your new business will consume you if you are not careful. You are the only one who can take the time to relax, to exercise regularly, and make sure the business doesn't cost you your relationship with your family.

No business is worth the expense of a divorce. Take today and walk the beach, a shaded trail, or go shopping for whoever suits you- the clothing store or the hardware store. None of it matters unless you have fun doing it.

Michael Gerber, in his famous book E-Myth, talks extensively about working in your business instead of ON your business. He means that you can do more in the long run if you put your feet up once in awhile and consider how best to manage your business instead of spending all your time doing the work of the business.

Take the time today to consider how best to structure your business so that you can spend more time ensuring it grows instead of trying to do every possible part of the business yourself.

NOTES:

DAY 10

Car signage

A car sign can be an incredibly easy way to get potential clients to call you. If your sign is done right- and few are. Ensure you have them on both sides of your vehicle and a small single line with your phone number and 'home watch service' on the back.

Most car signs are so poorly done, they never work. Here are some simple Do's and Don'ts that you should follow:

DO remember how many car signs you have read. Not many, right? Because they are too busy, too small, unreadable, or all of the above.

DO invest in some research before heading off to have your sign made. Cheapo Internet magnetic signs will bake and break.

DO remember that 'pretty' and 'effective' may not be the same, and many times, are the opposite. Simple is king here. Your business name or logo is not what people buy. "Home Watch Service 123-456-7890" is much more effective than most signs.

DO use your area code, since your clients may live in another state and use the cell number from that area, not yours.

DO put at least your phone number on the back of your vehicle. Remember, your vehicle moves. Door signs will only be seen when stopped in traffic.

DO make the most important information largest. Your phone number; what benefit you offer.

DO price graphics applied directly to the vehicle instead of just magnetic signs. They look better and last longer. Go to a local sign shop and ask.

DON'T forget that you have your phone number on the back of your car. Drive like a maniac and expect to get phone calls - from those you cut off...

DON'T believe that people will call because of the name of your company. They won't. They are much more interested in what you do or how you can save them time, money, embarrassment, or sleep.

DON'T make the name of your company the biggest part of the sign.

DON'T put a picture on the sign unless you are using the entire side of your vehicle.

DON'T make all the type the same size.

DON'T use a dark background and white letters. It's hard to read and most people won't. Remember the simple sign thinking.

DON'T Use light letters on a light background. Again, no one will be able to read it.

DON'T get cheap magnetic signs. They are thin, easily crack, and can stick to the car in heat. Better to pay more for a good magnetic sign than a cheap one.

A good set should run about $125 per set, while direct apply graphics can be the same price or sometimes even less.

NOTES:

DAY 11

Pricing

Pricing your services is one of the most challenging parts of the business. You can price too low and be forever behind. You can price too high, although this is very unusual.

There are only three ways to determine the price:

> Guess. Just make up a number. Not my idea of a great way, but many people do it this way. Then after you find out you are making about $5 an hour for your work you can try and raise prices. Good Luck.
> Do what your competition is doing. Another poor way. Chances are they are not making any money. Besides, how did they come to their rate? Probably used #1...
> Base it on VALUE you give. Instead of trying to charge by the hour, make your service so much better that homeowners would naturally want to use you. Then you can charge higher prices. Also target nicer homes, where your services are needed to prevent BIG losses. Believe it or not, many people will pay more if they think you will do a better job. (I charged $150 per month and no one ever complained!!)

Remember this formula, too:

Total Revenue = number of clients x monthly charge

Sounds simple right? But it isn't. The reason is the more clients you have, the more time you need to take care of the properties.
So let's look at the typical case of someone who charges $50 and has 25 clients. The total per month is $1250. If you need three hours per house per month, including transportation,(pretty efficient operation), that's 75 hours. Although the math looks good at $16.00 an hour, it doesn't make economic sense because
1. You have to subtract the cost of the gas/car mileage, supplies, and

other material
2. You have to subtract for advertising, Internet, telephone, etc.
3. You have to pay taxes from that amount.

Now that $16 an hour looks pretty slim.

As a minimum, I recommend you plan to make at LEAST $25 an hour for your work. It should and can be much higher if you operate efficiently and market properly.

So the best way to increase the money coming in, is to charge more because you offer a premium service.

Now look and see what 25 clients would be if you charged $100 a month. Now you have the same investment of time and materials, but you are grossing $2,500 a month. You have money available for extras, like flowers when your clients come home, Thanksgiving cards, and other niceties. You can also market your services better because you make enough to have some money to do it right.

There is no simple pricing plan but from my experience, most services are not charging enough. It reflects in their service. And they get the cheapie clients who whine a lot. Trust me on this point- charge more and provide a HUGE value and you will have loyal clients...

NOTES:

DAY 12

Credit cards or cash and checks?

Although cash and checks sound nice, they have a very high time factor- you need to go to banks routinely, have to worry over them bouncing, have to sort through mail to match them up with clients, keep track of who paid and who didn't, etc.

The time you spend in this business must be managed. How much time will you spend trying to track down a client who hasn't paid his invoice yet. If you go to the bank today, you will get checks in the mail as soon as you return from the trip. Oops- another trip. All of this is solved when you make everyone use credit cards.

With credit cards, you are in control. Sure, they cost you a few bucks for processing, but adjust your rates to cover it and it will save you HOURS and hours of problems. Get the number- and the expiration date- during the initial 'service agreement' signing. If they are concerned that you have their credit card number, remind them that they are giving you the keys to their entire house!

Get paid up front
Professionals collect their fees up front, before they work. I recommend you control the money flow. DO NOT send invoices waiting for your clients to pay. Instead, send invoices on the 1st of each month and let them know they will be billed on their credit card each month on the 5th. Just explain this is how you do your business. If they don't like that, they can find someone else!

Credit cards are the most common way of handling money. I recommend using something simple like Propay® or a similar 'enter the numbers using your computer' company. These businesses specialize in handling credit card transaction for smaller transaction accounts like you will have.

Your homework is to set up a credit card acceptance plan.

NOTES:

DAY 13

Get into the conversation

You can go into this business completely alone, if you want.

Never talk to another businessman, pretend there is no one else in the same business, and hide in your office.

Sadly, your efforts will mean you do a lot of things wrong, waste money, have problems others have solved, and spend more time re-inventing things than you ever spend growing your business. You are doomed to either failure or smallness.

One way to solve this is by 'staying in the conversation'. This phrase, which I learned from Sales Trainer Extraordinaire Eric Lofholm, really makes sense. I have learned a lot from others. It has saved me hundreds of hours of time. I can discuss my problems with others and get a different perspective on problems and solutions.

There are other business people in your local Chamber of Commerce. The web is full of sites with people in the home watch business. Their numbers are growing all the time. There are also associations forming all the time trying to get everyone together. I do not take a stand on any of these- you have to research and make the choice.

But you need to find other people who are in business to stay motivated, help you solve problems, and to exchange ideas.

Your homework is to use the local agencies and web to find someone to keep you in the conversation.

NOTES:

DAY 14

Advertising and Marketing

We could spend several weeks on this topic alone, so this is merely an overview.

The basics are three simple steps
> Create an appealing message
> Identify who your market really is
> Decide what media is best to approach them

Create an appealing message
Your goal is to think like your customer or client. What worries them about leaving a house empty? About leaving it to the neighbors? Have they had bad experiences? Do they know their insurance changes when the house is empty over 30 days? Do dome research and then write a message that addresses their needs and desires. It may take many messages, as some will resonate and some won't, depending on each person.

Indentify Your Market
As part of the first few day's activities, you found several ways to find potential clients. Now is your time to further refine that list. Does your newspaper list recent house sales? If so, you may have an especially ripe list- those new to the area. They are more likely to hire a service than use neighbors they don't know well.

Choose the media
A website is a minimum, but what do you use to drive people to the website? I have used:

Postcards. Simple to make and easy to mail. Make sure each one has an easy way to contact you (website and phone number are great) and also a reason to contact you now. Maybe a special bonus, 'call before we fill up for the season', etc. (I never discount my services, so I do not recommend giving a month of free service or similar discounts.)

Lumpy Mail. I have sent offers in pills bottles ("Is your empty home giving you a headache?), sent aspirin in a letter, and even heartburn pills. Anything you send that is lumpy will get opened much more often than a flat envelope.

Multiple letters. People are so busy that they are rarely interested immediately. I sent a series of three letters, each one calling out more problems and offering more bonuses. Some people recommend up to 9 letters, but three will work in most markets if written well.

Home Shows. I have done them and don't recommend them. The cost is high and results few. Most people who go to home shows are not multi-home owners so you are shouting to thousands of people unqualified for your service.

Referrals. I always asked new clients to give me the names of people they think could also use this service and usually got at least one or two to add to my marketing list.

'Five around' marketing. Whenever I signed up a new client, I had a reason to write to all the neighbors. By merely telling them I was now handling the property in the owner's absence, I had a reason to give them my card and a brochure. If one or more of them travelled, too, I could count on getting a call.

Brochures. Everyone asks for a brochure and 99% will never use them. If you have the time to write one, DO NOT put prices, exactly what you do, etc. The brochure should be used to get them to call you for all the information- not be a substitute for that call. You also must make the brochure 'evergreen', that is, it should be able to last for a couple years. The last thing you want to do is have a brochure that is outdated within a month of having it printed.

Your primary job is to market and sell your new business services.

Marketing is everything you do to make it appealing. It's also everything you do that involves advertising, promotion, and Client Oriented Thinking®. Let's look at some of the most obvious and then talk about some other ideas.

We discussed uniforms. The more professional your business appears, the more trust you build. Car signs fit into this category. Your mannerisms, like taking your shoes off when entering a property, or buying little booties to go over your shoes. Carrying a clipboard and taking notes. Using your camera or phone to record specific items of note when touring the property.

Your phone message leaves a big impression. Crying kids in the background of a recorded message ruin it. So does "This is Jim, leave a message." Make it professional.

Key security. How do you protect your clients' keys? Leaving them in your car with the name and/or address is not safe. Once you design the method, use that in your marketing.

Always have a Welcome Home Card for their arrival. I always had flowers arranged through a local florist.

I had a complimentary grocery shopping offer before clients came home.

The list of what you can do to differentiate your business from every other is endless. Think what would make the arrival special and make them want to come to you every year. That will build up your reputation and make existing clients extremely loyal.

NOTES:

DAY 15

Checklists

The one way to ensure you never miss an item is through checklists. It keeps you and your employees honest and also gives your clients confidence that checks are actually accomplished.

There are two kinds of checklists that will ensure a smooth operation.

Administrative checklists are used to ensure there is a system for everything you do. When you interview a new client, how do you remember everything? The special instructions for the burglar alarm, the phone number for the lawn service, who to call if you see insects? You need a *New Client Checklist*.

How do you ensure you get your new clients into your system? Programming your cell phone, starting a file, adding them to the emergency call system—an internal checklist.

When clients leave your care? You need a checklist to ensure the keys are returned, the account is charged, and any credit card numbers are destroyed.

All of these are administrative checklists.

Operational checklists used to do the actual work. Consider a separate checklist for each of the following events:

Closing - used the first time you survey a property after the owner has departed for the season. You ensure everything is ready plus you fully understand the differences of this house versus others.

Opening - a checklist to ensure the house is opened properly for the owners arrival at the end of the season, for a visit, etc. You would hate to have your clients arrive home to find the water off, all the blinds closed, and the air conditioner set too high. You want them to arrive home as if they never left, and this checklist ensures it gets done.

Routine - This is the most often used checklist. Your weekly/biweekly visits use this to ensure all the grounds are checked, the house exterior, interior, appliances, humidity, vehicles, etc.

Pre-storm - If you live in an area that has violent weather, and almost everyone does from blizzards to hurricanes, you need a checklist that ensures you do specific items. For example, if you live in a hurricane prone area, you may have to install shutters, remove lawn furniture, etc.

Post Storm- Anytime a storm hits, you may need to survey your properties to ensure everything is fine. A blizzard can cause power outages, roof leaks, and frozen pipes. Simple summer storms in Florida can cause power surges that fry air conditioners, open electric garage doors, or interfere with pool equipment.

You should be able to make your own checklists but some may be available on the Internet as well. Your checklists should cover all the normal and routine services like plumbing, heating, air-conditioning, appliances, temperature, humidity, power equipment, and automobiles.

Also the doors, windows, locks, burglar alarms, and water leak checks. The outside should also include cleaning up if needed, mail, trash, etc.

In my service I used my own checklists that were then modified for each property. One may have had a vehicle that needed checking, while another had a water softener. One had a pool, while another had 4 AC units.

Whatever you do, ensure you keep a record each time you visit or it could come back to bite you when an issue arises.

NOTES:

DAY 16

At the beginning of the book I emphasized that I am not an accountant. This especially applies to this section. Make sure you check everything here with your personal accountant if you have a question.

Taxes
Why would you need a whole day to consider taxes? There are several reasons:

- If the business makes money or loses money, it affects your taxes owed
- Depending on the form of business, the income or loss of the business 'passes through' or becomes part of your 1040 Internal Revenue Service Form.
- If you have employees, you will probably have payroll taxes that must be paid quarterly.
- Tax problems can bring the business down faster than???

Do I need an accountant? What is the difference between an accountant and a bookkeeper? Are there alternatives when I am first getting started?

Record keeping plans
Receipts in a box is a poor way to do business. Software alternatives.

Two ways to write off vehicles - Standard deduction and actual expenditures. Remember I am not a lawyer nor accountant so make sure you run any of this information through one or both of these.

Importance of records
No matter which system you choose to use, actual expenses or standard deductions, you must keep very accurate records. Depending on the maintenance of your vehicle, the age, and

the miles per gallon, one or the other system should be better. For my work, the standard mileage computation was optimal as it saved me from intense record keeping and allowed me to carry a small booklet, available in most office supply stores for less than $5. This is a record of your business miles, making life simpler. You simply record the miles, multiply by the government's rate for the period, and that is your expense.

NOTES:

DAY 17

The key to marketing is to meet the needs of your prospective clients by solving their problems, eliminating what keeps them up at night.

Advertising and marketing:
Don't be a marketing victim! Everyone and his brother trying to sell advertising will contact you. Chances are they will not understand your business, will promise fantastic results, WIL NOT guarantee results, and are more than willing to take your money.

I recommend direct marketing- spending all your money only against a very targeted and select group using direct mail. Advertising on large media outlets like TV and radio are wasted dollars since most of the people hearing your ad do not care since they are not your perspective clients.

My most successful campaigns targeted new people. By getting them interested before the neighbors convince them to leave the house to them. Lists are available for purchase, possibly from the local taxing agency, or through realtors. My experience has been realtors are not a good source, though.

On day 1 you started building a list. I recommend you use a method from a very well known and successful marketer Chet Holmes who used a top 100 program. Go after the top 100 (or even 50 if you are truly money limited) with a hard campaign until they either buy or die.

This book is written only to get you started.

There are many more topics that will help you expand your business and income. These items include subjects like:

Advanced Marketing Techniques like home shows
Newsletters sent monthly are a huge loyalty builder
Catalog of Services that can be used to make more money

Referral programs to get your clients to refer others.
Testimonials from clients to use on your website
Literature - how to create brochures and other sale pieces.
Managing your time using software- and smart phones
Weather Problems- how to address emergencies
Optional services to increase your income and client happiness
Initial set up fees- an extra source of income
Year round fees to ensure clients return

Some of these topics will be available in the future. Check back at www.39pageguidebooks.com.

NOTES:

DAY 120

Why would I have a day 120 in a book on starting in 17 days?

Because there is so much more to learn. This is a BONUS section with hints for making the business less time consuming and easier to run.

Software
There are many ways to use software. I love my smartphone and combine it with the many apps that are offered.

Client Management
You can keep all your info in your office or have access to it from anywhere. One of the easiest Client Resource Management (CRM) programs is Salesforce.com. They have a very inexpensive 'contact manager' that is great and accessible via smart phone. Need the phone number for the preferred plumber for Mrs Smith? You can find it instantly on site and call directly.

Billing
I use Quickbooks online and added the credit card billing feature once I got bigger. When I started out, I used Propay.com until I outgrew it.

Managing surveys
I used Formstack.com to build all my checklists into forms that I could access on the road. Then I just checked off the items and, when finished, it automatically sent a copy to my office email for my records. I started out using paper forms, but outgrew them quickly.

Dialmycalls.com
A great way to get information out to all your clients at once. Once you program all the numbers you want dialed, you can call from anywhere, talk the message, and your voice is now sent to each of

the phones. Pretty cool. Saved me a ton of time during storms and other emergencies and clients loved it.

Standardized email responses

A huge time saver is template emails. I sent out emails before people left, before they arrived home, to thank them for joining, etc. I made up a template that had everything but their name. It was set up to be personal because their name was in several places, but it was a 1 minute operation when I needed to do it instead of spending 10 minutes drafting a new one each time.

How to keep clients forever

If you look at the pricing and implement the other ideas in this book, you should be able to charge a fair amount that give you the ability to do things no one else ever does. That is what keep people coming to you- the pain of leaving is too much. Here are my top methods to do that:

Flowers on arrival

Women love flowers and their husbands don't ever buy them often enough. I always have fresh flowers on arrival. I have a deal with a local florist that I will order all my arrangements from them at a fixed price if they continue to give me great service. I buy over $3000 of flowers a year so I get some pull. Include a Welcome Home Card that you personally sign.

Thanksgiving cards

Your competitors may send Christmas cards. Just hope your clients are Jewish, Muslim, Jehovah's Witnesses, etc. On the other hand, no one send Thanksgiving cards! Aren't you thankful for the business and their trust? Say it!

Coffee cakes

In Florida, January is the time everyone finally relaxes. They are in their winter homes, the holidays are over and they are relaxing before heading up North again. Every year, I send a coffeecake to their house that says "Enjoy this on a relaxing morning now that the holidays are over. A gift from HomeWatchValet." They cost less than $30 and everyone who got one renewed with me for years.

Anniversary cards
A simple anniversary card noting the anniversary of them using your service is a great way to communicate.

These are the tip of the creative iceberg. Think of your own ways. A client who stays with you cost nothing in marketing. New clients cost a lot, so work to keep your existing clients harder than getting new ones.

NOTES:

ABOUT THE AUTHOR

Mark Mehling is a serial entrepreneur who started HomeWatchValet in 2005. After retiring from the military, he continues to fly as a commercial pilot, and sees the world through the lens of marketing.

Using the marketing materials and results from HomeWatchValet, he was "Marketer of the Year" finalist for Glazer-Kennedy Insider's Circle, now GKIC, a 25,000+ group of business owners from all over the globe intent on growing their businesses by following the methods of Dan Kennedy. As a trained copywriter, he also is a member of the American Writers and Artists (AWAI) Circle of Success. His book, *"Leaving Your Home-ALONE,"* is the leading publication for information on leaving property empty for months at a time.

In his business, HomeWatchValet, Mr. Mehling still has some of his original clients from his first year in 2005. Most of those clients whose property he no longer watches have moved, sold their home, or passed away.

Mr. Mehling started HomeWatchValet in 2005. While walking his beautiful dog, an Akita named Zoie, he came upon an empty home with water seeping from the garage. The neighbors knew nothing. No one knew how to contact the homeowner. No one had a key.

Mr. Mehling and the neighbors watched helplessly as water came from the garage. When someone finally broke a window on a door at the side of the garage, they gained access only to find a broken water softener line had flooded the 'sunken' living room.

After filling up, it started draining to the garage where it slowly went down the driveway. There was at least $20,000 damage according to a friend who was involved with the cleanup.

Mr. Mehling knew there had to be a better way. Thus was born

Home Watch Valet.

Mark Mehling is also the author of *"LEAVING YOUR HOME-ALONE, a step-by-step guide to leaving a property vacant for months at a time,"* available on Amazon.com.

www.ingramcontent.com/pod-product-compliance
Lightning Source LLC
Chambersburg PA
CBHW060633280326
41933CB00012B/2028